- VETERINARIAN GUIDE

TORTOISE CARE
A Guide From A Veterinarian
On Caring For Your Tortoise
Make Your Tortoise Live For 50 Years Or More

DONALD WILSON

Tortoise Care : A Guide From A Veterinarian On Caring For Your Tortoise

Make Your Tortoise Live For 50 Years Or More

By: Donald Wilson

TABLE OF CONTENTS

Table of Contents

Publishers Notes

Dedication

Chapter 1- What You Need To Know About A Tortoise Before You Buy One As A Pet

Chapter 2- Best Type Of Pet Tortoise To Buy : Different Species And Which One Makes The Best Pet

Chapter 3- Creating The Right Environment For Your Tortoise : Providing A Good Habitat

Chapter 4- What To Feed Your Pet Tortoise To Make Live Longer : The Best Food And Schedules To Feed Your Tortoise

Chapter 5- How To Monitor The Health Of Your Tortoise : Common Health Issues And How To Treat Them

Chapter 6- Which Other Pets To Put In With Your Tortoise : Fish And Tortoise Are They A Good Combination

Chapter 7- Breeding Your Tortoise : How To Find The Right Mate And The Process

Chapter 8- Tortoise Owner Tips

About The Author

Publishers Notes

BINDERS PUBLISHING LLC

Disclaimer

This publication is intended to provide helpful and informative material. It is not intended to diagnose, treat, cure, or prevent any health problem or condition, nor is intended to replace the advice of a physician. No action should be taken solely on the contents of this book. Always consult your physician or qualified health-care professional on any matters regarding your health and before adopting any suggestions in this book or drawing inferences from it.

The author and publisher specifically disclaim all responsibility for any liability, loss or risk, personal or otherwise, which is incurred as a consequence, directly or indirectly, from the use or application of any contents of this book.

Any and all product names referenced within this book are the trademarks of their respective owners. None of these owners have sponsored, authorized, endorsed, or approved this book.

Always read all information provided by the manufacturers' product labels before using their products. The author and publisher are not responsible for claims made by manufacturers.

The statements made in this book have not been evaluated by the Food and Drug Administration.

Binders Publishing LLC

7950 NW 53rd Street

Miami,

FL 33166

Kindle Edition 2012

BINDERS PUBLISHING PRESS is a trademark of Binders Publishing LLC.

For information about special discounts for bulk purchases, please contact Binders Publishing Sales Department at 646-312-7900 or publishing@binderspublishing.com

Designed by Colin WF Scott

Manufactured in the United States of America

DEDICATION

I want to dedicate this book to all the pet owners that have a tortoise and he or she is like a part of the family. Here is to making your tortoise live longer.

CHAPTER 1- WHAT YOU NEED TO KNOW ABOUT A TORTOISE BEFORE YOU BUY ONE AS A PET

I usually advise that whichever animal you are thinking about bringing into your home as a pet, that you do the necessary research so that you can learn all you can about their needs and what you need to do to care for them. When this is done, you will be able to decide beforehand as to whether or not you will have the time and the monetary resources that to make both you and your pet's experience in your home a healthy, fun and happy one. Animals do a lot to enhance the lives of human beings, but if you are not prepared to look after them it can be a burden on you and an injustice to them.

One of the very first things I tell persons who are thinking of purchasing a tortoise as a pet is that if you are considering keeping them in doors, you will need to give this serious thought, as a majority of them do grow to a size that may not be comfortable for keeping them indoors after a while. The truth is that they do grow slowly, but between five to ten years they experience a significant growth spurt. As such, when you are researching the species of tortoise that you want to become a part of your family you should look for the size they usually grow to. If you want to keep your tortoise indoors, then I would suggest that you get the ones that will remain on the smaller side, like the Egyptians, Red Footed, Russians, Marginateds and Hermanns.

However, if you live in a climate that is warm, this will enable you to keep your tortoise outside for most of the year, or even all year round if you so desire. In this case you will be able to choose from any one of the species that you are considering. You would need to think careful about the right climate as well as about the space you will need for them outdoors.

Another option is for you to keep the animal indoors when it is a baby and then set up its home outdoors. Large tortoises tend to not be too fond of being cooped up indoors and they do not like small spaces either, as I learnt from personal experience with my own tortoise. However, if you do not have the ideal temperature indoors, smaller tortoises will also be affected.

When you bring your tortoise home they may seem a little stressed. This is normal however, as they are transitioning to a new home so they may seem out of sorts for the first twelve to twenty four hours. Giving him a soak in shallow warm water will usually perk them up. They may not eat for the first day or so as well. Be sure that you have their habitat set up before they come home so that their transition can be as comfortable as possible.

CHAPTER 2- BEST TYPE OF PET TORTOISE TO BUY : DIFFERENT SPECIES AND WHICH ONE MAKES THE BEST PET

Some of the best tortoises to purchase as pet are the Egyptians, Russians, Marginated and Red Footed. The Russian tortoise is popular as a pet mainly due to their size and their hardiness. They range in size between five and eight inches as males and six to ten inches as females. The males usually have a longer tail that is tucked to the side and the females' shells have a flared scute.

They live for an extremely long time; approximately seventy five years and are very social with human beings. They can be kept both indoors and outdoors. However, they may fall prey to other animals; even your dogs, so you have to ensure that their habitat is very secured if you will be keeping them outside. They are very good diggers, and as such you have to also make sure that their pen is built deep down into the ground. They usually hibernate during the winter months and are herbivorous.

The Egyptian tortoise us one of the most beautiful tortoises there is. They are called the golden beauties and is an endangered species.

They should not be mixed with other species as they are very sensitive to the disease the other species carry. They aestivate during periods that are dry and hot, but they do not hibernate. They make good pets but you will need to be especially careful with their housing and food and they have to be handled carefully.

Even though the Marginated tortoise is the largest of the European tortoises, it is still considered to be a small tortoise. They range in size from ten to twelve inches and the tails of the males of the species are longer than that of their female counterparts.

The males are usually longer, but the females still tend to outweigh them. They earn their name by the marginal scutes that are extended near to their hind legs as adults. They have an oblong shell and a thickness around their middle. They hibernate in winter and are herbivorous.

The Red Footed tortoises usually live until they are fifty years old and sometimes even longer, and therefore, like their counterparts you will need to be prepared to take care of them for the long haul. They usually grow to between ten and fourteen inches in size but can sometimes grow to as big as sixteen inches and even more.

There is also a smaller species that is called the cherry-head that grows to between ten and twelve inches and approximately thirty pounds. There are sometimes referred to as Savanna or redleg tortoises. Its name is derived from the orange or red scales that are visible on their limbs and they are very popular as pets even though they are protected under the Convention on International Trade in Endangered Species (CITES).

CHAPTER 3- CREATING THE RIGHT ENVIRONMENT FOR YOUR TORTOISE : PROVIDING A GOOD HABITAT

Most tortoises will adapt easily to its surrounds, whether it is one that is physically built or one that is natural. However, for those that are man-made there are certain considerations that have to be made such as the convenience of cleaning it, a place where they can hide when they want to and enough space for them to live comfortably in. They can live both indoors and outdoors depending on the temperature in your house and the climate in which you live.

You should try to capture as much of the features of the natural habitat as possible such as the lighting and the humidity so that they will not feel too out of place and will stay healthy. A humidity of between twenty and thirty percent is usually good for most species of tortoises that are being kept in captivity. They will need ultraviolet B lighting and temperatures of 80 F in the day and 72 F in the night.

They do not usually bask on the open ground, so you will need to provide them with a cluster of low-growing, sturdy plants in their basking area and they will need a shallow water bowl in their habitat with the sides being low enough so that they can reach into it. Tortoises do not swim so you need to be careful that the water level is easily accessible but that it is not deeper than their bridge.

For the Egyptian tortoise (also called the Kleinmanni) you will need to provide them with light for twelve hours of the day and they also need a sufficient number of spots in which to hide so they do not become too stressed. For a single Egyptian tortoise, a single Egyptian tortoise should have a habitat that is three feet by two feet and not less than eight square feet for a pair, with an additional 2 to 4 square feet being added for each additional tortoise that you add to the enclosure.

Some good substrate for their habitat include peat moss, scattered gravel and sand as well as compact sand. A material that is completely opaque should be used for their sidewalls. Their enclosure walls should be at least eight inches high, and this seems to be an ideal height for my little Egyptian tortoise. This prevents them from climbing out of the enclosure. The interior should have sufficient ultraviolet lighting that you can get from a powerful UV Mercury vapor lamp.

For a single baby Marginated tortoise, his cage can be as small as thirty or forty gallon long (some people say twenty) but I would recommend that it be thirty or forty gallons. You can have two Marinated tortoises living comfortably and stress free in a forty gallon cage. However, a seventy five gallon (or bigger) cage would be ideal for adult tortoises.

They enjoy digging, so a thick layer on substrate one side of their cage and a thin layer on the other would be ideal. For their outdoors habitat, as it is for most tortoises that are housed outdoors, this can be simple.

Basically their environment has to be enclosed to keep out other animals that may harm them and secured, as they are little escape artists.

CHAPTER 4- WHAT TO FEED YOUR PET TORTOISE TO MAKE LIVE LONGER : THE BEST FOOD AND SCHEDULES TO FEED YOUR TORTOISE

In addition to where you house your tortoise, what you feed them is also very important in order to maintain their health. There is a general list of foods that tortoises eat and enjoy and then there are foods that are necessary for specific species. The general lists of foods include grape leaves, the flowers and leaves of the Hibiscus, dandelions, grass and weeds from your garden. squash (banana squash, summer squash, and yellow crookneck squash), zucchini fruit and leaves, wandering jew, nasturtium, the flowers and young leaves of roses, aloe vera and the pads and fruits of the cactus.

In addition to the above, you can also occasionally treat them with endive, broccoli, collard greens, tomatoes Romaine lettuce and corn on the cob. They can also be specially treated with strawberries and apples, but make sure the seeds are removed and all these foods are free of pesticides. They also need calcium; especially hatchlings and females. As such, you should sprinkle their food with carbonate or crushed egg shells. Tortoises should never be fed spinach, peas, beans, cat food, bananas, iceberg lettuce, Chard, any kind of sprouts, cabbage, or watermelon.

Marginated tortoises are opportunistic in their eating, so they eat whenever food is available to them. This is so because they are never too sure as to when they will be fed again. In captivity they will eat a number of different commercial foods as well as natural plants, but their preference is fruit (some fruits) and leafy greens.

However, they will also eat red leaf, green leaf and Romaine lettuce, mustard, turnip and collard greens, kale and parsley. They do eat cabbage as well, but I would recommend that this only be fed to them sparingly as if fed too much and over the long term, it can negatively impact on the thyroid.

The foods for Egyptian tortoises must be high in fiber, rich in calcium and low in protein. This diet will help significantly with their growth and the proper functioning of their digestive tract. Avoid giving them fruits as the sugar is not very good for them. If they are kept indoors, they should be given additional calcium supplements with D3.

A Russian tortoise likes to graze and loves eating broad leaf plants. The best diet for a Russian tortoise is one that is a mixture of flowers and leaves. Their favorite food is dandelion. They usually eat a lot of food over a short period of time. You can feed them radicchio, endive, chicory, Romaine lettuce, red and green leaf lettuce, turnip and mustard greens, cabbage (occasionally) and Escarole. Unlike some species of tortoises they do not like eating the same thing day in and day out, they prefer a variety.

You can also choose to feed them ice plants, the flowers and leaves of the hibiscus, mulberry leaves, henbit, the leaves and flowers of the rose and cornflowers. You should never feed them fruits, Bok Choy, grains, iceberg lettuce and meat.

CHAPTER 5- HOW TO MONITOR THE HEALTH OF YOUR TORTOISE : COMMON HEALTH ISSUES AND HOW TO TREAT THEM

One you have decided to take on a tortoise as a pet, their health now becomes your responsibility. You have to pay close attention to them as they are actually programmed to hide their illnesses as this is what they usually do when they are in the wild so as to avoid being preyed upon. It will be necessary for you to do routine health checks so that you can pick up on any health issues they may be having so you can take them to the veterinarian to get taken care of.

Your tortoises should be checked to ensure that their eyes are bright as this is usually an indication that they are keeping good health.

There are also ways in which you can prevent illnesses if you adhere to what has been addressed in previous chapters relating to the proper nutrition, caging, humidity and heating as this is crucial to the prevention of common illnesses in your tortoise. The foregoing plus consistently keeping their cage clean will prevent both you and your tortoise from getting and spreading salmonella. In addition to being prone to salmonella, tortoises are also quite susceptible to respiratory and parasitic infections. They should get their fecal checks to ensure they are parasite free, and if they are showing signs of respiratory infections, then they should be taken to the veterinarian.

Tortoises sometimes have a tendency to become stressed and when this happens their levels of activity as well as their health can decline. Do not overcrowd their habitats and avoid having them be handled by small children who will drop them when they are scared by a sudden movement of the tortoise.

They will also suffer from too long toenails, a broken beak and also penal prolapse. If you keep them on dirt substrates then this will help to sufficiently wear down their toenails and this issue will be taken care of. A broken beak usually rebuild naturally after a period of time. You would only need to seek the assistance of a veterinarian only if it starts to grow back in a way that is abnormal.

Male tortoises often get penal prolapse. If this happens to your tortoise then the tortoise will need to be soaked so that when the penis becomes moistened, the dirt around his penis will be washed away from the tissues. I suggest you use either warm water or saline solution to help the tissue to shrink. You should never push back the tissues and a veterinarian should be consulted if there is no shrinkage in the tissues.

Bacteria, lowered temperatures and stress that causes the immune system to become lowered are the major causes of respiratory illnesses in tortoises. If they are having respiratory issues then they will be wheezing and there will sometimes be a mucous discharge coming from their mouth and/or nose. You should not wait until your tortoise has to be breathing from its mouth to take him to the vet, as this means the respiratory illness has progressed to a serious stage. The tortoise should be taken to the veterinarian early and the stage if the infection will determine whether they will be treated with a nebulizer and/or antibiotics which may be administered via an injection or through the nose. Once it is caught and treated early, the tortoise should recover fully.

They are also prone to shell rot. Bacteria and fungus are the main cause of shell rot. The bacteria will usually get into the tortoise's body via a scrape, a cut or from lesions on the shell of tortoise. Septicemia; an infection of the bloodstream may result if shell rot is not treated early. Early rotting of the shell will begin with flaking, pitted or white powdery patches on the shell. The vet will have to take care of the shell rot and you will need to ensure that the enclosure for the tortoise is sufficiently dry.

Chapter 6- Which Other Pets To Put In With Your Tortoise : Fish And Tortoise Are They A Good Combination

As previously discussed, tortoises are prone to stress, and one of the factors that cause them to be stressed is overcrowding in their enclosure. As such, whichever other creature or creatures you decide that you want to live with your tortoises or tortoise. If this is eliminated, this will greatly diminish the risk of them becoming too stressed.

One of the biggest issues you will face when trying to make the decision as to which animal to house with your tortoise is if they will require the same temperature, lighting, space etc so that they can live together with both creatures getting all they need to keep them healthy and happy.

I find that tortoises can live by themselves and be quite fine doing so. However, if you have decided that you do want to add another tortoise to your family, do what I did; get a tortoise of the same species or sub-species.

You will need to monitor them to make sure they are not showing each other any type of aggression as if they are, then you may need to separate them. In addition, it is important for you to quarantine your new tortoises for about 6 months so that you can ensure it is completely healthy before housing it with your other tortoise or tortoises.

When tortoises of different species are placed in the same housing facility, there will be a great risk of them transferring infections and other diseases. On top of the risk for disease transference, there is also the issue of the increased stress that housing another tortoise with the one you originally had, can cause. This should be given serious consideration as when a tortoise becomes too stressed it causes a suppression of the immune system, making it prone to illnesses.

If you have a small tortoise then it may be safe to keep a goldfish or bigger species of fish with your tortoise. Otherwise, fishes may get eaten by the tortoises. Even though I have not personally kept a fish with my tortoises, I know people who have successfully housed the two and have done so for many years.

CHAPTER 7- BREEDING YOUR TORTOISE : HOW TO FIND THE RIGHT MATE AND THE PROCESS

Breeding tortoises is often not as straightforward as just putting a male and a female in the same place during mating season and leaving them to let nature take its course. You will need to give serious thoughts to those overly-amorous males that will harass a female tortoise if you only have one female tortoise in with the male. If she gets fertilized she may not want to lay her eggs with the male constantly being a pest to her. I suggest that if you will only be mating one female and one male, that they be kept separately and then you supervise the mating process.

It would be smarter for you to put 2 or 3 females in with the male so that his exuberance be divided between them. You should never cross-breed your tortoises as different species have different habits with respect to mating, there is a very high risk parasites being transferred from one species to the next and the chance of normal and healthy fertilization of these eggs will be very small.

Breeding may take place between June and March, but usually happen more frequently between September and November. After the tortoises have mated; between September and December, the female will begin walking all around her enclosure or tank looking for a suitable place in which to nest. She will find between 4 or 5 places and then abandon them before finally deciding on the location that she sees fit to lay her precious eggs, even though the site she will finally decide on is usually one of the sites she has tried out. She will start with the usual pallet digging, but will end up using her hind legs to dig out her nest. The digging generally lasts an average of 5 hours and when the next has been dug, she will begin laying an egg every 3 minutes.

She will then fill in the nest after all her eggs are laid. The eggs will be incubated under the ground after about eight months or if you have to move them for whatever reason, they can be placed in an enclosed container that is half filled with vermiculite and water with a 1-1-2 ratio in weight for the vermiculite and the water. The enclosed container would have to be opened once a week to give the eggs fresh oxygen. The eggs are usually incubated between 82.5 and 84 F and hatching usually happens in a temperature of between 118 and 156 days after the eggs were laid. However, some eggs may be hatched after 92 days.

For specificity with different species of tortoises, breeding techniques for Greek tortoises and Spur-Thigh tortoises would vary since they do originate from different environment and may hibernate and estivate at different times. The spring time is when they will breed and some of them will dig a well formed nest and cover their eggs completely, while others will make a slight depression in the ground and sprinkle the dirt over their eggs.

CHAPTER 8- TORTOISE OWNER TIPS

Tortoises can be fun animals to keep as pets, but you have to be willing to do the work necessary to keep them healthy and happy. In addition to all you have already learnt about tortoises from the previous chapters, there are many other important information that will help you in a significant way in your journey with your pet tortoise.

For instance, because they carry all their weight on their very small legs, when they end up in an upside down position, then they will not be able to flip themselves over ad can end up dead if they are exposed to too much sun and become overheated. The Padlopers may be the only species that can flip themselves over as they weigh less and their legs are both stronger and longer.

In addition, even though the shell is tough, the tortoise does feel your touch as their shell is male from the same keratin; the same protein that makes up the nails of a human being. Furthermore, they do not breathe like other animals do due to the fact that their shell is too hard to expand for them to inhale. As such, your tortoise inhales by contracting its muscles so the body cavity is enlarged and exhales by pulling in its legs so that there is a reduction of the body cavity and by contracting its internal muscles so its organs are forced against the lungs and the air is forced out. Tortoises are fascinating creatures. Learn all you need to learn about them and enjoy the great experience of being a tortoise owner.

ABOUT THE AUTHOR

Donald Wilson loves animals, especially guinea pigs, turtles, bearded dragons and tortoises. He was an only child but he never craved another sibling due to the fact that he always had animals around him. He always wanted a turtle or a bearded dragon as a child but his parents decided that they were much too busy to spend the time that was needed to care for these animals, and he was too young at one point, and then way too busy himself with both school and athletics by the time he got to the age where he was old enough to look after one. As such, it was not until he was out of college and settled in his career that he decided to get not one, but two turtles; a Red eared Slider and a Painted Turtle and one male and one female bearded dragon and then later added two guinea pigs and one male and one female tortoises to his list of pets. He knows all there is to know about all these animals and enjoys sharing his vast knowledge about them with all those who are interested in learning about these creatures just for their general knowledge but also those who are considering them as pets. He sees his tortoises and turtles as his lifetime friends as they are among the longest living creatures in existence and although they do take a lot of care, it is completely worth it to him. He also adores his friendly little bearded dragons that close their eyes when he rubs their heads and his lovable little guinea pigs that are always anxious to cuddle in his lap..

Printed in Great Britain
by Amazon

Praise for
GROW with Goals

Doyin does not write about theories. Her words come from a place of practical insights and results. 'GROW with goals' is a comprehensive how-to guide that if applied, will revolutionise your goal setting efforts.

Olawunmi Brigue
Transformational Coach
Editor of GROW with Goals

Somehow, Doyin managed to put within this book what would take months of professional coaching and mentoring to unearth. It is a self-help book for anyone who has at least one thing to improve upon. It's the kick on the 'backside' I've been waiting for!

'Bisi Olonisakin
Risk consultant

This book is absolutely brilliant. It brings goal setting and achievement to you in a way that is both proven (research based) as well as personal (with life application stories) whilst making it easy to remember the concepts and principles using acronyms. It is written in such a way that you cannot go wrong with your goals using it. I applaud the author and highly recommend this book

Freda Raymond-Obi
Life & Business Strategist